MAYA'S BiG FEELINGS

Stressed for the Test

Written by- Amy Elkins Dickerson, LPC, RPT

Illustrated by- Shruti Sharma

ISBN: 9798852895028

Dedication

For Mama, Dad, John and Sarah-
you've lifted me up with your love
and I am so very grateful.

Love you more... to the end of space and back!

This is Maya.

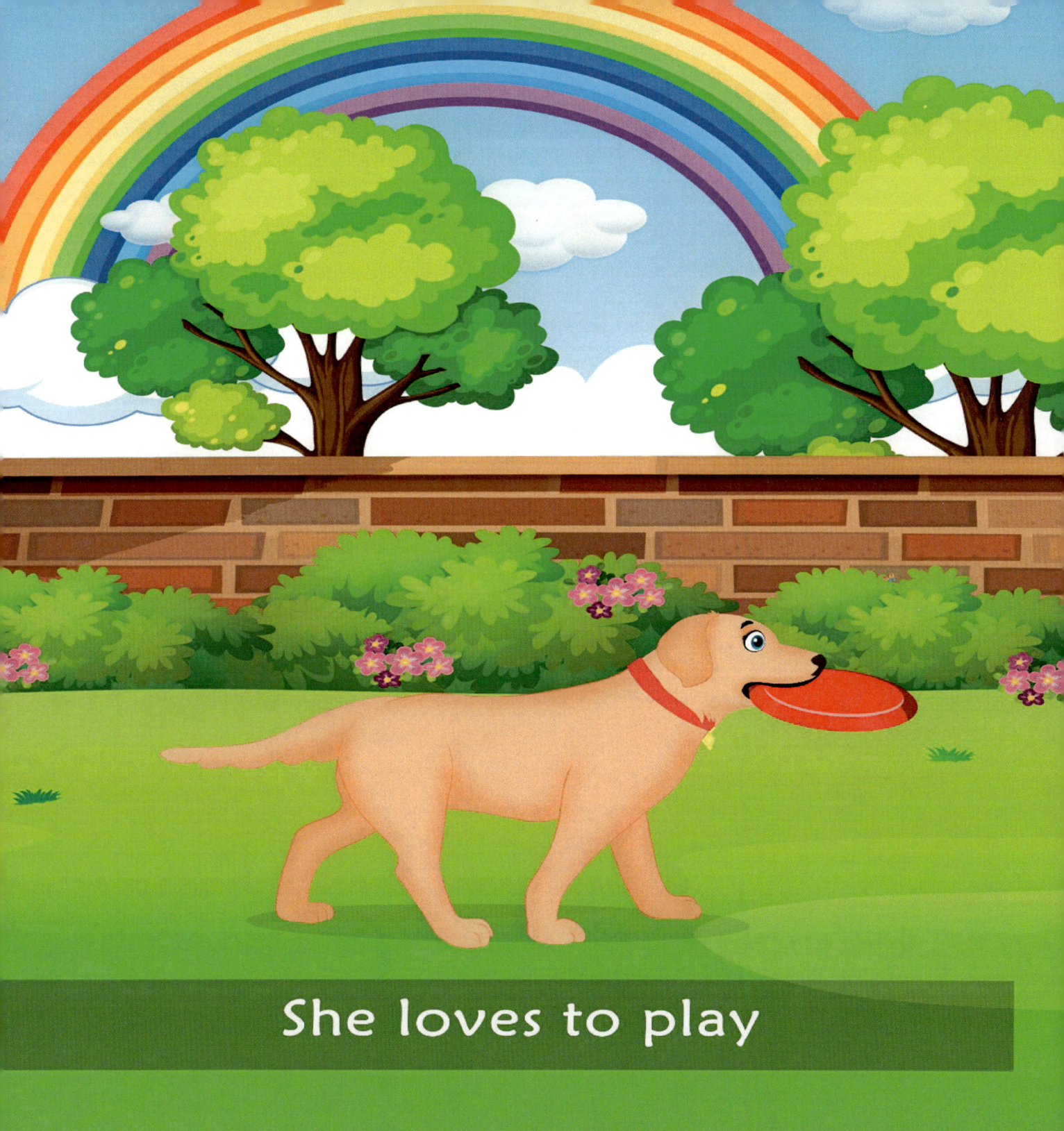

She loves to play

and eat

and snuggle.

Sometimes Maya has big feelings
that make her feel icky.

This morning, Maya woke up with a tummy ache.
She has a big test at school today and she is worried that she won't do well.

Maya is having some negative thoughts-
"I'll never get the answers right." and
"I'm not good at math."
She felt so worried that it made her not
want to go to school.

Maya's Mama noticed that something was not quite right.
She asked Maya "Maya, you seem to be a little worried. Is something on your mind?"
Maya thought for a second and said, "My tummy is hurting."
Maya's Mama said, "Sometimes when we are nervous about something, it makes our tummies feel kind of funny. I wonder if you are worried about something?"

Maya thought about it and said "I'm worried that I'm not going to do well on my math test today. I think that I'm going to get all the answers wrong. I'm no good at math!" Maya felt tears in her eyes and a lump in her throat.

Maya's Mama looked at Maya and said "Sometimes we have negative thoughts that aren't true that make us feel badly. I think that if you talk back to your negative thoughts, you will feel less worried."

Maya then said to her Mama "Well, I did study last night. So, maybe I'll do well. Even though math isn't my favorite subject, I work hard and do the best that I can."

Maya's Mama smiled and said "Yes! That is all true. I'm proud of you for talking back to your negative thoughts."

Maya seemed a bit worried still. Maya said "Mama, what if I get nervous before the test?" Maya's Mama said "Something that helps me when I feel nervous is taking big breaths. Let me show you."

"First, you breathe in deeply through your nose and let your belly get really big, kind of like you're blowing up a balloon. Then, you slowly blow out through your mouth and watch your belly go down, like the balloon is deflating."

Maya's Mama then encouraged Maya to do the deep breathing with her. After a few deep breaths, Maya's Mama asked Maya how she felt.

Maya smiled a big smile and said, "My body feels so calm, and my tummy no longer hurts." Maya's Mama smiled and stated "Great! You can do this breathing anytime, anywhere. Your breath is always with you."

With that, Mama noticed the time and said, "It's time to finish getting ready for school!"

Maya brushed her teeth, packed her bag and went to catch her bus.

Maya was so happy she shared her feelings with her Mama, and she was so glad that she now had a few tools to help herself feel better the next time she noticed she felt stressed.
So, remember, notice the sensations you have in your body, share them with a caring adult, talk back to your negative thoughts and use deep breathing the next time you feel stressed or worried.
If Maya can do it, so can you!

Note for Grown-ups

Oftentimes, when children in our care have big feelings, we may not know how to respond. Hopefully, this book helped guide you and the dear child in your life by providing new ways to identify, express and cope with emotions.

Identify: Reflect the emotion that you see in your child- happy, mad, sad, worried, or calm.

Express: Model how to express feelings by using phrases such as "I feel worried when..."

Cope: Encourage your child to engage in a calming activity whenever they are having a big feeling- belly breathing, taking a walk, drawing, and listening to music are all good ones!

More tips can be found by listening to "Little Ones/Big Feelings with Amy Dickerson" podcast which is available at:
www.aedpsychotherapy.com, Apple, Spotify and Amazon Music.

Additionally, if managing your child's emotions has become too overwhelming or if they are struggling to function in school, at home or with peers, please reach out to a local therapist. You don't have to do this alone!

Lastly, thank you for all that you do to help the children of today become emotionally intelligent adults of tomorrow.

About the Author

Amy Elkins Dickerson is a Licensed Professional Counselor in the State of Connecticut and a Registered Play Therapist. She is the owner of AED Psychotherapy, LLC, a private practice in New Canaan, CT. Amy earned a Master of Mental Health Counseling degree from Teachers College, Columbia University and a Bachelor of Arts in Creative Arts in Therapy and Psychology  from Russell Sage College. Amy lives in CT with her husband, John, daughter, Sarah and dog, Maya 😊.

Made in United States
North Haven, CT
29 August 2023